I0081669

From Struggle to Strength: The Journey of a Reverend

Rev Maxwell Ngove

Published by Bethel Publishing House, 2024.

FROM STRUGGLE TO STRENGTH: THE JOURNEY OF A REVEREND

First edition. July 18, 2024.

ISBN: 978-0796154460

Written by Rev Maxwell Ngove.

Table of Contents

Epigraphy 1
ACKNOWLEDGMENTS 3
DEDICATION 4
FOREWORD 5
PREFACE 6
INTRODUCTION 8
CHAPTER 1 10
The Plight of Orphans 11
CHAPTER 2 12
Rural of Rhythms 13
CHAPTER 3 15
A Journey through Rural Education 16
CHAPTER 4 18
Navigating Loss and Rejection 19
CHAPTER 5 22
Navigating the New Horizons 23
CHAPTER 6 26
Embracing Community at Church 27
CHAPTER 7 29
In the company of the Great 30
Napoleon Gomo 32
Rev. Peter Rore 33
Kudakwashe Gwemende 34
Bishop Trevor Manhanga 35
Mr. Watson Mlambo 37
Dr. Joshua Banda 38
Bishop Harrison Sakala 39
Coach J Dianne Tribble 40
Pastor Newton Festus 41
Professor Augustine Deke 42
CHAPTER 8 43

London Calling........ 44
CHAPTER 9........ 46
Northern Ireland........ 47
Encountering God........ 51
Navigating Distractions........ 52
CHAPTER 10........ 53
Return to Zimbabwe........ 54
CHAPTER 11........ 56
Meeting my wife........ 57
CHAPTER 12........ 60
The Art of Worship and Fasting........ 61
CONCLUSION........ 63

To all young people who find themselves navigating difficult circumstances. May they always remember that God's love and care transcend any challenge they may face, and may they draw strength from their faith to overcome adversity. To all who see their future as bleak and find themselves fainting in their walk of faith due to circumstances. And to my forever Heavenly Father, who became my ultimate source of strength when I never saw anything meaningful in my future after losing my mother and not knowing my father.

FROM STRUGGLE TO STRENGTH

The Journey of a Reverend

REV. MAXWELL NGOVE

FROM STRUGGLE TO STRENGTH

The Journey of a Reverend

X

Rev Maxwell Ngove

Author

Epigraphy

"But they that wait upon the Lord shall renew their strength; they shall mount up with wings as eagles; they shall run, and not be weary; and they shall walk, and not faint." - Isaiah 40:31 (KJV)

REV MAXWELL NGOVE

ISBN: 978-0-7961-5446-0

Edited by – Tanea Nyika & Patience Sakutukwa

Layout by – Bethel Publishing House

Cover Design- Lindani L. Thango

Published at Bethel Publishing House

Printed in South Africa

Scripture and quotation are taken from:

AMPC 1987. The Lockman Foundation

KJV Cambridge. University Press

NLT. 2015 Tyndale House Foundation. Illinois

ACKNOWLEDGMENTS

I extend my deepest gratitude to my late grandmother, Margaret Mahlangu (Mbuya Gwande), whose unwavering love and strength shaped my character and guided me through life. Though she is no longer with us, her legacy lives on in my heart. I also want to express my heartfelt appreciation to my beloved mother, the late Beaula Ngowe, whose sacrifices and endless support paved the way for my journey. Additionally, I am grateful to my loving uncle, Godwell Ngove, and his family, for their encouragement and assistance along the way. Special thanks to Bishop Chivimbiso Ngowe and his family, my late mother Florence Ngowe Chirisa, Pastor Patricia Chijiri, and Greater Mhuru for their invaluable support and guidance throughout my life's journey. A heartfelt acknowledgment goes to my wife, Winterpet, and my children, Righteous Inzwirashe Ngove and Kaylie MakatendekaIshe Ngove, for their unwavering love, understanding, and encouragement. They are my pillars of strength and constant reminders of God's blessings in my life. Lastly, I would like to recognize the efforts of Tanea Nyika, Patience Sakutukwa and Bethel Publishing House, whose editing prowess and dedication were instrumental in bringing this work to fruition. Your contributions are deeply appreciated.

DEDICATION

To all young people who find themselves navigating difficult circumstances. May they always remember that God's love and care transcend any challenge they may face, and may they draw strength from their faith to overcome adversity. To all who see their future as bleak and find themselves fainting in their walk of faith due to circumstances. And to my forever Heavenly Father, who became my ultimate source of strength when I never saw anything meaningful in my future after losing my mother and not knowing my father.

FOREWORD

Reverend Maxwell Ngove's life story is the ongoing narrative of how God captured his heart in extreme adversity and showed Maxwell all His goodness. This incredible story is about a life well surrendered to God. When I first met Maxwell, I drove through his town of Mutare, Zimbabwe, with my wife and another Pastor. The old car we were driving had broken down. We decided to stop and ask Maxwell to help us. Not knowing each other, he willingly offered his vehicle to us. Before we left Mutare, Maxwell asked me to return and minister in his school ministry and church.

COVID-19 came that year, and we were physically separated but not spiritually. We met Maxwell again on Zoom and began to pray as a global team worldwide. Since that day, we have continued to meet daily for prayer. Maxwell has shared his vision for his city, his school outreach, and his music ambitions. He has accomplished his goals amid COVID-19, economic despair, health challenges in his family, and personal loss. What impresses me about Maxwell is the joy of the Lord, which shines through in his beautiful smile. He exemplifies the words of Nehemiah, *"The Joy of the Lord is My Strength".* I eventually returned to Mutare and saw God work through Maxwell and his ministry. He showed me his land and shared his vision. It will come to pass.

As you read this amazing story, you will learn that Maxwell is not defined by his life's challenging circumstances but by God's goodness.

Mike Maddy

Founder and President, Bold Faith Christian Movement

PREFACE

"And Jonathan, Saul's son, had a son who was lame in his feet. He was five years old when news of Saul and Jonathan came from Jezreel, and his nurse picked him up and fled. But as she hurried to escape, he fell and became lame. And his name was Mephibosheth." - 2 Samuel 4:4 (KJV) when we examine the story of Mephibosheth, certain aspects of his life strike a chord with many, including myself. Initially, he was not afflicted, but tragedy befell him when the kingdom came under attack. Similarly, many of us were not born into poverty, sickness, or rejection, yet life's circumstances can abruptly alter our trajectory. Perhaps a beloved family member perished in conflict, a father abandoned his responsibilities, or mental illness struck our children. These unforeseen trials are not inherent to our existence but are imposed upon us along life's journey. The adversary has a cunning way of sowing seeds of doubt and despair in our minds.

Moreover, my own journey mirrors Mephibosheth's in many ways. From the humble beginnings of rural life, I found myself thrust into the spotlight of newspaper headlines in Northern Ireland during my early days in ministry. It was a miraculous journey, one only made possible through the guiding hand of God.

Yet, my path was not without its trials. I emerged from a life overshadowed by rejection, where anger and bitterness threatened to consume me upon discovering my father's abandonment of our family. As I reflect on these challenges, I am reminded of the resilience that faith provides in the face of adversity. As I embark on penning this book, "From Struggle to Strength: The Journey of a Reverend," I am compelled to share my story. For me, there exists no more potent illustration, definition, or demonstration of God's favor and grace than the narrative of my own life. Through the lens of my experiences, I hope to offer solace and inspiration to those who find themselves grappling with their own trials. This book is not just a recounting of personal struggles, but a testament to the transformative power of faith and perseverance.

In the pages that follow, I will delve deeper into the challenges I faced, the lessons I learned, and the blessings I received along the way. It is my sincere hope that my journey will resonate with readers from all walks of life, and that together, we may find strength and encouragement in the unyielding love of our Creator.

My existence epitomizes God's grace to those who know me intimately and, perhaps, to you, the reader, as you delve into these pages. This book is dedicated to those who have struggled to grasp their divine purpose, who have found themselves teetering on the edge of despair.

INTRODUCTION

Born into poverty, I faced hardships that would have broken many. Village life was harsh, with every day a struggle for survival. The crackle of firewood and the flicker of oil lamps were the constants of my early years. Yet, my spirit remained unbroken. Raised without my father, and later losing both my mother and grandmother, left a void, a lingering bitterness as I yearned for guidance and nurture that was never fully realized, despite my mother's best efforts. Still, a dream was harbored—a vision of something greater beyond the confines of my village.

Moving to the city, the marvels of modernity astounded me. Upon my arrival in Norton, wearing oversized shoes that symbolized my humble beginnings, I was thrust into a world vastly different from the one I had left behind. From indoor plumbing to the marvel of television screens, the urban landscape both dazzled and bewildered me. Imagine a rural boy arriving in town, surprised to find a toilet inside the house or discovering that sadza could be cooked with electricity instead of firewood. Seeing animals on a television screen for the first time, I believed the snake on the screen posed real danger in the house. The electric stove, a simple appliance to many, was a source of amazement, as I was accustomed to cooking over open flames. These encounters symbolized the new world I had stepped into, a world full of possibilities that once seemed unreachable.

The city, a place of contrasts, was where dreams faced the harsh realities of urban life. Moving to the urban areas brought hope, light, and a fresh start, igniting a transformative journey. Yet, it was here that faith shone brightest. Solace was found in the belief that God had a plan, even when the path was obscured by shadows. Through the trials, strength within was discovered, a resilience forged in the crucible of adversity. Amidst the wonders of modernity, the lessons of resilience and community ingrained in me during my rural upbringing served as guiding beacons, navigating me through the tumultuous transition.

FROM STRUGGLE TO STRENGTH: THE JOURNEY OF A REVEREND

This journey is one of profound introspection and self-discovery, marked by moments of joy and sorrow, triumphs and setbacks. Above all, it is a journey fueled by unshakeable faith—a faith that sustained me through the darkest times and propelled me towards a brighter future. This is the story of my life, a life of defying the odds, emerging from humble beginnings in rural Zimbabwe to become a beacon of hope and inspiration for countless individuals.

The journey from struggle to strength is not just a personal odyssey but a testament to the power of perseverance, the importance of community, and the transformative impact of faith. It serves as a reminder that, in the midst of adversity, there is always hope. And that, with faith as a guide, any obstacle can be overcome.

Dear reader, join me on this journey—a journey of struggle, resilience, and ultimately, strength. Within these pages, you will find not just a story, but a message of hope—a message that reminds us that, no matter how dark the night may seem, the dawn will always break, and with it, a new day filled with endless possibilities. Welcome to "From Struggle to Strength: The Journey of a Reverend." As you turn these pages, may the tale of rising above circumstances inspire you. My unwavering faith carried me through valleys and led me to mountaintops. This is not just my story; it is a story for all who dare to believe in the God of impossible.

CHAPTER 1

The Plight of Orphans

"Life is not about waiting for the storm to pass, but learning to dance in the rain." - Vivian Greene

In recent research, Zimbabwe has emerged with a notable orphan hood rate of approximately 35%, while Africa as a whole holds a rate of around 34%. Globally, the prevalence of orphans is significant, with an estimated rate of 33% and steadily increasing. These figures underscore the widespread impact of orphan hood, portraying the challenges faced by children who have lost one or both parents and must navigate life's uncertainties without familial guidance and support. As I reflect on my journey as an orphan, memories flood my mind like an unstoppable tide. I recall the first time I entered a new home, timid and uncertain, greeted by the unfamiliar faces of strangers who would soon become my family. "Welcome," they said, their voices tinged with warmth and curiosity. Little did I know then the trials and triumphs that awaited me within those walls. In Zimbabwe, family is the cornerstone of society, a source of strength and stability in the face of adversity.

From a young age, I learned the importance of community and the bonds that unite us, transcending blood ties to form a tapestry of shared experiences and mutual support.

Through the lens of orphan-hood, I discovered the true meaning of resilience. Each setback became an opportunity for growth, each obstacle a stepping stone on the path to self-discovery. Empathy and compassion, once abstract concepts, became my guiding principles as I navigated the complexities of life without the guiding hand of my parents. The journey of an orphan is one of profound challenges and unexpected blessings, a testament to the resilience of the human spirit and the transformative power of love and community. As I continue to forge my path in this world, I carry with me the lessons learned from my journey, embracing each moment with gratitude and determination to make a difference in the lives of others who walk a similar path.

CHAPTER 2

Rural of Rhythms

"The ultimate measure of a man is not where he stands in moments of comfort and convenience, but where he stands at times of challenge and controversy." -Martin Luther King Jr.

I made my entrance into the world not in a sterile hospital room, but within the comforting walls of a humble home on June 26, 1973, in Matuku Village, Zimbabwe. Growing up amidst the simplicity and warmth of rural life, our family dwelling stood nestled beside the serene Dzidze River. Nature's cadence dictated our daily routine, from bathing in its waters to guiding cattle across its banks. In this idyllic setting, I grappled with the introspection and shyness that often accompany rural childhoods, navigating the vast expanse of nature's embrace. The future seemed uncertain, with little clarity beyond the rhythms of community existence. Despite aspirations of finding employment, opportunities were limited to roles tied to rural livelihoods, perpetuating the cycle of simplicity.

In the rustic charm of rural life, I observed the allure of local beer halls and the camaraderie of communal gatherings. Despite these temptations, I remained steadfast, guided by a sense of divine preservation through the trials of adolescence. Though my understanding of the gospel was limited, church attendance provided a semblance of spiritual grounding amidst the chaos of rural life. Each Sunday, the Anglican Church offered refuge from the distractions of earthly pursuits, serving as a reminder of the dichotomy between spiritual and earthly matters.

Reflecting on those formative years fills me with awe at the journey from rural obscurity to the precipice of possibility. God's unseen hand guided me through the uncertainties of life, lifting me from the depths of self-doubt and illuminating a path filled with purpose. Life in rural

Zimbabwe is characterized by resilience and humor, where laughter thrives despite adversity. Despite the simplicity, there lies a lack of ambition and aspiration, with academic pursuits often taking a backseat to agricultural activities. For those whose academic endeavors falter, solace can be found in the familiar rhythms of agricultural life. However, limited opportunities for upward mobility lead many to seek escape in alcohol, further perpetuating a cycle of stagnation. Despite the challenges, the tranquility of the Dzidze River remains a constant source of solace, echoing with the whispers of nature and the wisdom of generations past.

As I reflect on my upbringing, I find myself yearning for the simplicity of rural life, where contentment is found in life's basics and blessings are cherished.

CHAPTER 3

A Journey through Rural Education

"Education is not the learning of facts, but the training of the mind to think." -Albert Einstein

In the heart of rural Zimbabwe, education was revered, yet its transformative potential wasn't universally acknowledged. Reflecting on my upbringing, I recognize the profound impact it had on shaping my young mind. Even before reaching school age, I was given the moniker *"chidhikoni"* (short man) by the village, a title steeped in skepticism about my work ethic. My days were spent tending to cattle, plowing fields, and undertaking various agricultural tasks, instilling in me a strong sense of responsibility from an early age.

Life in our village was a rich tapestry of simplicity and communal joy. We delighted in traditional drinks like *"mahewu"* and found solace in spirited soccer matches with makeshift balls. The journey to Saint Paul's Kuimba Primary School, a ten-kilometer trek each way, underscored our unwavering commitment to education, even in the face of the harsh realities of walking barefoot on cold, wet ground during winter.

My early school years were fraught with challenges. Clothing was a luxury, and I often wore hand-me-downs that swamped my small frame, serving as a constant reminder of our modest circumstances. Despite my grandmother's efforts to introduce me to Sunday school, my confidence waned in the classroom. I withdrew from speaking up, fearing ridicule from my peers, exacerbating my insecurities.

As I progressed through the grades, my self-esteem continued to plummet, adversely affecting my academic performance and participation in extracurricular activities. Puberty ushered in a new set of challenges, and I sought refuge in channeling all my energy into my studies, determined to validate my worth through academic excellence.

In a surprising twist of fate, I emerged as the top student in my class during the second term of Grade Seven. The accolades and acknowledgment from my peers provided a much-needed boost to my confidence, reaffirming that success was attainable, despite the formidable obstacles in my path.

As the results of the final Grade Seven Exams were announced, I found myself among the select few who had excelled, a testament to resilience and determination in the face of adversity. Though my early years of schooling were rife with hardship, they were also punctuated by moments of communal solidarity and resilience-building activities, each stride forward a testament to the unwavering spirit of perseverance.

CHAPTER 4

Navigating Loss and Rejection

"When one door closes, another opens; but we often look so long and so regretfully upon the closed door that we do not see the one which has opened for us." - Alexander Graham Bell

As I approached the culmination of Grade Seven, the trajectory of my life veered sharply when my mother relocated to Toronto Township in Mutare and remarried. However, tragedy struck swiftly when she became the victim of a fatal accident, leaving me under the care of my grandmother in the village. The news of her untimely passing reached me indirectly, shattering my world and rendering me vulnerable and adrift. The solemn reality of my mother's demise descended upon me with crushing force as mourners gathered at my grandmother's homestead. Amidst the lamentations of grieving villagers, I grappled with the enormity of my loss. Questions about my future reverberated through the air, enveloping me in a shroud of uncertainty and trepidation. As the funerary rites unfolded, familial discussions ensued regarding my fate. I sat silently beside my grandmother, a mere spectator to the shaping of my destiny. The burden of rejection and abandonment weighed heavily upon me as the course of my life lay precariously in the hands of others.

Despite the overwhelming sorrow and ambiguity, pockets of solace emerged as elder women extended their comforting arms and offered words of support. Yet, the path ahead loomed dauntingly, punctuated by the void left by my mother's absence and the nebulousness of what lay beyond the horizon. Yet, amidst the darkness, faint glimmers of hope began to flicker, serving as a reminder that even in the throes of rejection, unseen doors await to be opened.

Grandmother's kitchen.

The place hut which Pastor Maxwell Ngove was born and raised.

As my mother's passing cast a shadow over our humble abode, the weight of my future rested heavily on the shoulders of my family. Within the stifling confines of my grandmother's hut, relatives deliberated my fate, their accusatory glances branding me as an unwanted burden. Amidst the turmoil, my uncle Godwell emerged as a beacon of hope, extending his hand to welcome me into a town life in Norton with the ache of living my grandmother behind.

With the finality of my Grade Seven examinations behind me, preparations for my journey to Norton unfolded swiftly. The prospect of leaving behind the familiar comforts of my rural home stirred within me a potent mix of excitement and dread. Despite tearful pleas to remain by my beloved grandmother's side, the inevitability of departure hung heavy in the air, casting a somber shadow over my heart. As I bid farewell to the only life I had ever known, the specters of survival and separation haunted my young mind. With each step toward the unknown, the ache of leaving my mother and grandmother behind intensified, threatening to engulf me in a tumultuous sea of uncertainty. As I embarked on my secondary education at Vimbai High School, the challenges of urban life tested my resolve. From missed enrollment opportunities to comical mishaps with oversized shoes, each setback served as a poignant reminder of the resilience forged in the crucible of adversity.

Despite the mockery and laughter that trailed behind me like a persistent shadow, I refused to be defined by the rejection of my past. With each stumble and misstep, I pressed onward, embracing the opportunities that lay before me with unwavering determination. Reflecting on the trials and triumphs of my journey, I am reminded of the sage words of Alexander Graham Bell: "When one door closes, another opens." Though rejection may have cast its long shadow over my early years, it ultimately paved the way for the resilience and fortitude that would carry me through the challenges that lay ahead.

CHAPTER 5

Navigating the New Horizons

"Education is not the learning of facts, but the training of the mind to think." -Albert Einstein

Approaching my high school education filled me with a sense of curiosity and determination, unlike anything I had experienced during my primary schooling. High school represented an advancement—a platform for broader learning and the development of critical thinking skills. I realized that education held the key to overcoming challenges and unlocking my full potential. My high school journey spanned from 1988 to 1991, a period marked by significant growth and discovery. By the time I reached Form Two, I found myself gradually acclimating to urban life. I forged friendships with peers who shared my commitment to education and aspirations for the future. Among them were Charles, Stephen, Edward Siyabonga, Dick Labu, and many others. Together, we formed a cohesive team driven by a shared dedication to academic excellence and personal growth. I cherished the bonds of friendship that blossomed during this time, as we spent countless hours studying and engaging in discussions about life's complexities. Our collective pursuit of knowledge fostered an environment where intellectual curiosity thrived, and the exchange of ideas fueled our aspirations for the future.

Norton with friend, Daniel Makaza (right) who led to me to Christ.

During this time, my group of friends served as a source of motivation and support, urging me to remain steadfast in my pursuit of education. One of them was Daniel, who became one of the best friends who contributed to my salvation. His invitation to join him at the local SDA church marked the culmination of the Gospel he had been sharing with me their encouragement helped me to overcome the doubts and negative projections that some villagers had cast upon my future during my early years. I sat in the church as a visitor listening and then word was shared and sharply it penetrated my heart. The preacher warmly invited those who wanted to revive Christ. And he even said I know there is someone who is here who knows definitely that this is their day *u.mmmmm.* No longer confined to the stereotype of a mere cattle herder, I began to see God's hand shaping my destiny in remarkable ways. Amidst my studies, my uncle often took me back to the rural area to visit my grandmother. Norton had become a central meeting point for the Ngove family, with my uncle assuming the mantle of family responsibilities. These visits provided invaluable opportunities for familial bonding and discussions about important matters concerning our lineage.

During this period, my uncle also assumed the role of a mentor, guiding me with wisdom and practical skills. He taught me the fundamentals of gardening, chicken farming, and household chores, instilling in me a sense of industriousness and self-sufficiency. Despite the occasional ridicule from classmates over the red oxide staining my knees from polishing floors, I remained grateful to my uncle and his wife for their care and guidance.

As the years passed, my responsibilities expanded to include a milk business introduced by my uncle. The early mornings began at 4 am, as I set out to purchase milk from the nearby Kintyre Estate. Laden with two cumbersome 25-liter containers, I braved the cold mornings, often staggering under the weight of the load.

Despite the physical strain, I persevered, selling milk to local shops and on the streets before and after school. Though my peers often laughed or expressed pity for my endeavors, I took pride in contributing to my uncle's modest resources through this venture.

While some of my peers ventured into relationships with girls, I remained reticent, grappling with feelings of low self-esteem. An attempt to pursue a schoolgirl ended in embarrassment when another boy intervened and stole her attention away. This setback reinforced my resolve to focus solely on my education and personal growth, though the experience left a lasting mark of humiliation.

CHAPTER 6

Embracing Community at Church

"There are no strangers in the house of God, only friends we have not met." - William Temple

The year 1989 etched a significant moment into the fabric of my life—a moment of profound transformation and spiritual awakening. It was the year I was born again, surrendering my life to Jesus Christ. Days melted into weeks, and weeks into months, each marked by its own rhythm until fate intervened, steering me towards an encounter that would forever alter my path.

In the midst of the ordinary, a friendship blossomed with a boy named Daniel, a neighbor from the streets of Norton. His invitation to join him at Fatherhood from God SDA church marked the culmination of the gospel he had been sharing with me. Growing up without the presence of my biological father, Daniel's discussions about God the Father struck a chord deep within me. For years, I had longed for paternal guidance, and in that moment, I found solace in the realization that God was the Father I had been searching for all along. My first visit to Daniel's church felt divinely orchestrated, with the preached gospel aligning perfectly with our discussions.

On that fateful day in 1989, I made the decision to accept the Lord as my personal Savior, setting the course for a journey of spiritual growth and faith. Three years later, in 1991, God's hand intervened once again as I successfully passed my Cambridge Ordinary Level examinations. However, financial constraints thwarted my plans for further education, leading me to seek employment in Shamva at the invitation of my aunt, Florence Chirisa.

My two years in Shamva were marked by challenges and introspection, as I navigated the unfamiliar terrain of farm life amidst a backdrop of moral decay. Prayer and worship emerged as steadfast companions, providing solace and strength in the face of adversity. Through prayer, I sought divine guidance at every turn, while worship became a profound expression of my faith, offering a conduit for experiencing God's grace and comfort.

Amidst the trials, a providential encounter led to employment in the realm of computers—a field previously unknown to me. Despite lacking formal qualifications, I embraced the opportunity, guided by a newfound sense of purpose. Yet, my newfound employment was short-lived, leaving me once again adrift in uncertainty. In the face of upheaval, I turned to prayer, finding solace in the belief that God was guiding my steps, even in the midst of adversity.

Each trial became a testament to the unwavering faith that anchored me, reinforcing my conviction that divine providence was shaping my journey every step of the way.

Shamva Dapp Forest Estate

CHAPTER 7

In the company of the Great

"Life is either a daring adventure or nothing at all."
-Helen Keller

Trapped in the quietude of Shamva, a phone call from Mutare stirred the stillness of my existence. It was my uncle, Chivimbiso, reaching out from Salisbury, with a sudden recollection of my presence in the family. Inviting me to visit him in Mutare, he offered a glimmer of hope in uncertainty. Excited yet apprehensive, I pondered the significance of these continual journeys, wondering why fate kept leading me from one home to another.

Upon arriving in Mutare, the warmth of my uncle and his wife enveloped me, their joy evident at seeing me grow. Settling in Sakubva, one of Mutare's burgeoning townships, revealed the financial struggles my uncle faced as a pastor, with the church unable to provide sufficient support. Despite the challenges, they remained steadfast in their faith, opening their home to me amidst scarcity. During my time in Mutare, my spiritual journey took a profound turn under my uncle's mentorship.

Embracing new experiences and taking risks, I embarked on a path of self-discovery and growth. My days were filled with prayer, seeking solace and guidance in the bush, while my uncle imparted Christian fundamentals and exposed me to various aspects of ministry. As months passed without securing formal employment, I found myself increasingly involved in church activities, particularly youth ministry. Taking the helm of the youth department at Pentecostal Assemblies of Zimbabwe church, I introduced innovative programs that resonated with the younger generation, fostering growth and engagement within the congregation. The wisdom shared by American author Helen Keller rang true in my heart, reminding me of the transformative power of embracing life's adventures. Each encounter, each experience, and propelled me forward on my journey of faith and self-discovery. Along the way, I crossed paths with individuals who left an indelible mark on my life, shaping my personal and ministerial development.

Napoleon Gomo

Napoleon Gomo, the Director for Scripture Union in the Eastern region. It was under his guidance and leadership that my passion for children's ministry was ignited, setting me on a path of service and dedication to the youth.

Napoleon Gomo exemplified familial love and support, creating an environment where individuals could thrive and grow in their faith. His commitment to nurturing young leaders and empowering them to make a difference in their communities was truly inspiring. Under his mentorship, I learned the importance of compassion, patience, and unwavering faith in God's plan. In the company of great men like Bishop Trevor Manhanga and Napoleon Gomo, I found not only mentors but also lifelong friends and spiritual guides. Their wisdom, humility, and love continue to shape my ministry and my life, reminding me of the profound impact that one individual can have on the lives of others.

Rev. Peter Rore

Reverend Peter Rore is not just a leader in children's work; he's a dynamic force that embodies the perfect blend of firmness and compassion. His leadership style is a testament to his unwavering commitment to the ministry and his genuine love for children. Under his guidance, I learned the importance of serving wholeheartedly, channeling passion into action, and leading with empathy. His mentorship has not only shaped my approach to ministry but has also inspired me to cultivate a deeper sense of compassion and understanding in all aspects of my life.

Timothy Tavaziva

Timothy Tavaziva is more than just a supervisor and mentor; he's a pillar of support and a beacon of encouragement. His dedication to his professional duties is matched only by his genuine care and concern for the personal welfare of those around him. Beyond offering guidance in the workplace, Timothy extends a helping hand, a listening ear, and a shoulder to lean on whenever needed. His mentorship has been invaluable in shaping not just my professional growth but also my personal development, instilling in me the importance of empathy, compassion, and integrity in all endeavors.

Kudakwashe Gwemende

Kudakwashe Gwemende is a leader of principles, a guardian of integrity, and a champion of family values. His unwavering commitment to upholding ethical standards and his steadfast dedication to nurturing familial bonds have left an indelible mark on my character and leadership style. Under his guidance, I've learned the importance of staying true to one's principles, even in the face of adversity, and the value of prioritizing family above all else. Kudakwashe's mentorship has been instrumental in shaping my moral compass and instilling in me a sense of responsibility to uphold integrity and honor in all aspects of life.

Bishop Trevor Manhanga

In 2007, during my ministerial journey in Manicaland Province, I had the privilege of getting to know Bishop Trevor Manhanga closely. It was a time of profound growth and transformation for me, returning to the province where my journey had begun eleven years prior as a volunteer and now assuming the leadership role. Truly, God's workings never cease to amaze me. Bishop Manhanga was more than just a figure in my life; he served as an instructor, a leadership coach, and a fatherly mentor. Spending time with him inevitably led to a sharpening of one's leadership skills.

I immersed myself in his teachings for several years, recognizing that this period was instrumental in preparing me for my future ministerial endeavors. Every Sunday, as Bishop Manhanga entered the sanctuary to deliver the Word, a palpable excitement filled the air. His sermons were not mere words but profound insights that dug deep into the essence of wisdom. He didn't shy away from rebuking, chastising, or comforting his congregation as needed. I vividly recall the year when our country held elections, a time of heightened anxiety for many.

Despite the uncertainty, Bishop Manhanga exuded hope through his ministrations, reminding us to place our trust not in election results but in Christ, the true hope of glory. His chosen song for that moment, *"How Great is Our God,"* resonated deeply with his message. Despite his esteemed position, Bishop Manhanga remained humble and grounded, traits befitting a true man of God. I distinctly remember one occasion when I drove him from Harare to Mutare in a small Raum vehicle. Despite his stature, he occupied the front seat with grace and humility. It was a journey of over 300 kilometers, yet every moment was filled with a profound sense of gratitude for the opportunity to serve and be in the presence of a spiritual giant. In Bishop Trevor Manhanga, I found not only a mentor but also a fatherly figure and a spiritual covering.

His influence on my life and ministry is immeasurable, and I am forever grateful for the privilege of knowing him.

Mr. Watson Mlambo

When I began my tenure as a coordinator in Manicaland, Mr. Watson Mlambo was simply a board member. However, he soon ascended to the position of council chairperson. I encountered Mr. Mlambo at Scripture Union upon my return from the United Kingdom. His demeanor was unique—a blend of composure, humility, and inner strength. In his presence, I found solace and warmth.

He possessed a genuine love for people, readily offering guidance and a listening ear. As a lecturer at Mutare Teacher's College and a former President of S.U., he also served as one of my mentors. During a particularly challenging time, when my family faced complications with our rented property after eight years of tenancy, Mr. Mlambo imparted invaluable wisdom. Despite the looming threat of legal intervention due to alleged non-payment of rent, his counsel resonated deeply with me. He advised, "This is the time to emulate Christ. Whether it means bearing the burden like the cross or settling dues, trust that God will provide in His own way." His words pierced through my doubts, offering a profound sense of healing.

Upon returning home, I shared Mr. Mlambo's counsel with my wife. Surprisingly, she echoed his sentiments, and together, we decided to pay the rent twice over and vacate the premises. Three weeks later, a former parishioner from Bulawayo, now residing in Saudi Arabia, unexpectedly reached out to us. In a gesture of kindness, he blessed us with the exact amount that had been disputed with our landlords. Through this experience, I learned the importance of embracing life's challenges and trusting in divine providence. Mr. Mlambo's wisdom and unwavering faith served as a beacon of light during a tumultuous period. His unique approach and presence continue to inspire gratitude in my heart, reminding me to patiently await the Lord's timing in all things.

Dr. Joshua Banda

Dr. Joshua Banda emerges as another pivotal figure in my ascent, extending a generous invitation for me to relocate to Mutare. Dr. Banda's support provided me with invaluable platfoms for growth and service, including opportunities within the missions in Zambia, where he currently presides as Bishop of the Pentecostal Churches. His guidance and mentorship opened doors to new horizons, amplifying the impact of my endeavors and fostering a spirit of collaboration and community. Dr Joshua is Zambian. He was a guest speaker in the church I pastored and he impacted me on missions and mentorship.

Bishop Harrison Sakala

Bishop Harrison Sakala occupies a special place, his presence a testament to the providence of divine connections. Our encounter, orchestrated by higher hands, unfolded with a sense of divine synchronicity as we had the privilege of hosting Bishop Sakala in Mutare. His ministry style resonated deeply with me, serving as both an inspiration and a source of guidance as I navigated the intricacies of my own calling.

Based in Lusaka, Zambia, Bishop Sakala's influence transcended geographical boundaries, enriching my journey with his wisdom and grace.

Coach J Dianne Tribble

Coach J Dianne Tribble is not just a mentor; she's a transformative force whose guidance in life coaching has opened new avenues of ministry and personal growth. Her unique approach to coaching combines wisdom, compassion, and a deep understanding of human nature, empowering individuals to unlock their full potential and live authentically. Under her tutelage, I've learned to embrace vulnerability, cultivate resilience, and harness my strengths to overcome challenges and achieve my goals. Coach Tribble's mentorship has been instrumental in helping me navigate life's complexities with confidence and grace, inspiring me to become the best version of myself.

Pastor Newton Festus

Pastor Newton Festus is more than just a pastor; he's a shepherd of souls, a beacon of love, and a source of unwavering encouragement. His genuine care for others and his steadfast dedication to the kingdom of God have left an indelible mark on my heart and soul.

Under his leadership, I've experienced the transformative power of love, witnessed the impact of selfless service, and learned the true meaning of faith in action. Pastor Festus's mentorship has been a guiding light in my spiritual journey, inspiring me to emulate his example of compassion, humility, and unwavering faith in God. Each of these individuals has played a significant role in shaping my journey, imparting invaluable lessons, and instilling in me the importance of community, connection, and continuous growth. Their mentorship has been a source of inspiration and guidance, propelling me forward on this daring adventure called life. In life's ebb and flow, these pillars stood tall, their support and guidance serving as beacons of light in moments of uncertainty and challenge. Through their wisdom, generosity, and unwavering faith, they have played a profound role in shaping the trajectory of my journey, infusing it with purpose, inspiration, and divine grace.

Professor Augustine Deke

In the tapestry of my journey, there are individuals whose presence and influence have left an indelible mark, propelling me forward on the path of purpose and growth. Among these pillars stands Professor Augustine Deke, a beacon of wisdom and insight whom I had the privilege of meeting at the 2021 SU conference. In his address on strategic thinking, Professor Deke illuminated the value of perspectives often overlooked, igniting within me a spark of inspiration.

His words resonated deeply, planting the seed of an idea that would later blossom into the decision to pen a book—a decision that would shape the trajectory of my journey in profound ways.

CHAPTER 8

London Calling

"Success is liking yourself, liking what you do, and liking how you do it."
-Maya Angelou

My journey of ministry continued to unfold as I dedicated myself wholeheartedly to serving God through the youth department at Pentecostal Assemblies of Zimbabwe. However, the beginning of 1996 brought about a significant turning point in my life as God opened a new door of opportunity for me. Scripture Union (S.U) extended an invitation for youth volunteers to undergo ministry training focused on children and young people in schools. Little did I know that this training would pave the way for a remarkable journey ahead.

Selected as one of the volunteers, I underwent induction training at the local S.U office in Mutare, which proved to be an eye-opening experience. Witnessing the struggles and challenges faced by children in schools ignited a deep passion within me for ministry. As I shared my testimony in various schools, I witnessed firsthand the transformative power of God's love and grace, not only in the lives of the children but also in my own. My involvement with S.U led to significant growth in our youth ministry at the local church, as the impact of our outreach efforts began to resonate within the community.

With each passing day, I found greater fulfillment and satisfaction in my work, realizing that true success emanated from within, rather than from external sources. Unexpectedly, an opportunity arose for me to share my testimony in schools in London, a prospect that seemed inconceivable given my humble background and lack of confidence. However, as events began to unfold rapidly, I found myself on the brink of a life-changing journey. Reverend Napoleon Gomo of S.U informed me of the invitation from London and advised me to prepare for the trip within eight months. Despite initial doubts and challenges, including the daunting task of raising airfares, I remained steadfast in my faith, trusting in God's providence. With the support of well-wishers and through fervent prayers, I persevered in my efforts to secure the necessary funds. However, as the deadline for purchasing the ticket drew near, my faith wavered, and negative voices threatened to overshadow my resolve.

Yet, just when all hope seemed lost, a miraculous donation arrived, precisely covering the cost of the airfare. It was a testament to God's faithfulness and provision, reaffirming my belief in His unfailing love and grace. With the ticket in hand, I embarked on the journey of a lifetime, bound for London to share my testimony with children in schools. The day of my departure arrived, marked by tearful farewells and heartfelt well-wishes from friends and supporters.

Accompanied by a few individuals from my church and S.U, I made my way to Harare International Airport, filled with a mix of excitement and trepidation. As I boarded the plane bound for London, I reflected on the extraordinary journey that lay ahead, grateful for God's guidance and provision every step of the way.

Upon landing at Heathrow Airport, overwhelmed by a flood of emotions, I marveled at the beauty of God's creation and the magnitude of His blessings. Tears streamed down my cheeks as I contemplated the journey that had brought me to this moment. Welcomed by a placard bearing my name, I was ushered into a new chapter of my life, filled with anticipation and gratitude. At London Bible College, I was greeted with warmth and hospitality, surrounded by fellow believers from around the world.

As I embarked on a mission trip to Northern Ireland, I embraced the opportunity to share God's love and grace with others, eager to witness His transformative power at work once again. My journey to London was not merely a physical voyage but a testament to God's faithfulness and provision. It was a reminder that with faith and perseverance, anything is possible, and that true success lies in following God's calling with courage and conviction.

CHAPTER 9

Northern Ireland

"If you have the words, there's always a chance that you'll find the way." - Seamus Heaney

My journey to Northern Ireland was marked by unexpected encounters and cultural adjustments. As I arrived at Belfast airport, I was greeted by Reverend Lowry, who welcomed me to this unfamiliar land. Amidst the bustling airport crowd, a mysterious Irish lady approached me with a warm greeting before vanishing into the sea of people. It was a moment of intrigue, leaving me pondering the possibility of divine intervention.

Transported to Green Island Carrick Fergus, I found myself immersed in the beauty of this picturesque locale. The Rector's residence, with its well-appointed rooms and lush surroundings, became my temporary home. As the only African in this predominantly Irish community, I faced the challenge of adapting to a new culture and deciphering the local accent. In the days that followed, I ventured out for my first shopping excursion, accompanied by the group I was to work with. Despite my apprehension, I was encouraged to select items of my choice, an experience both exhilarating and overwhelming.

The camaraderie of my companions eased my nerves as we indulged in a meal at a nearby restaurant before heading to the cinema to watch "Mission Impossible," a film that resonated with my sense of purpose and determination. My initial ministry outreach took place at Green Island Primary School, where I addressed the students during the morning assembly. Drawing from *Psalm 139:14,* I emphasized the message of self-worth and God's unique design for each individual.

Despite cultural differences and language barriers, my presentation was met with enthusiastic applause, reaffirming the universal truth of God's love and acceptance. Subsequent visits to schools such as Silver Stream Primary School and Carrick Fergus College provided further opportunities to share messages of hope and inspiration. Through familiar songs and heartfelt stories, I connected with the students, drawing upon my experiences in Zimbabwe to impart lessons of faith and resilience.

Reflecting on my journey from Zimbabwe to Northern Ireland, I recognized the hand of God guiding my steps and shaping my ministry. Each encounter, whether divine or mundane, served to strengthen my resolve and deepen my faith. As I stood in Richmond Park Gardens on my first day in London, I marveled at the path that had led me here, grateful for the opportunity to share God's love with others across borders and cultures.

My first day in London at Richmond Park

Newspaper Headlines

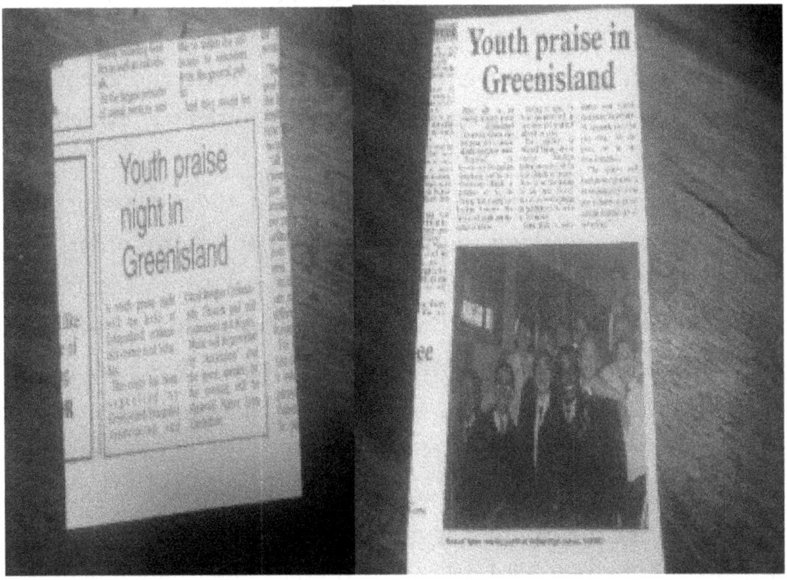

The unexpected turn of events during my time in Northern Ireland led to surprising newspaper headlines, marking significant moments in my journey of faith and ministry. My first experience addressing a high school assembly at Belfast High School filled me with fear and anxiety as I faced a large gathering of students. Despite my initial trepidation, I found the courage to deliver my presentation, relying on the guidance of the Holy Spirit. Little did I know that journalists were present, capturing the moment for local newspaper coverage.

The headlines featuring my story at Belfast High School left me incredulous, as I never imagined myself as newsworthy. With eager anticipation, I obtained a copy of the newspaper, feeling a sense of pride and gratitude for the opportunity to share my message with a wider audience. In the ensuing months, my story continued to make headlines in various local publications, underscoring the impact of my ministry efforts in Northern Ireland.

I was humbled to be recognized as a speaker at a musical concert, with one article describing me as "very good." The unexpected invitation to speak at the concert reflected the growing influence of my message and the receptiveness of the community. However, not all moments were marked by acclaim and recognition. During the concert, I encountered challenges as a group of disruptive students tested my patience and resolve.

In a moment of frustration, I confronted their behavior with a prayerful rebuke, invoking the name of Jesus to restore order. To my surprise, the following day brought news that the troublemakers had attended church for the first time, a testament to the transformative power of God's word. In the whirlwind of events, I was honored with the opportunity to officiate the opening of a community center, a role typically reserved for dignitaries and officials. The poster announcing the event, featuring my name and image alongside the Zimbabwean flag, symbolized the fulfillment of a childhood dream. Surrounded by journalists and dignitaries, I delivered a speech of dedication, reaffirming my commitment to God's calling in my life.

Encountering God

In the external accolades and accomplishments, I experienced a deep spiritual encounter that reaffirmed my sense of purpose and identity in Christ. One morning, overwhelmed by a sense of sorrow and longing for spiritual connection, I embarked on a solitary walk to the beach. Along the way, I encountered billboards bearing messages of God's love and sacrifice, serving as divine reminders of His presence in my life. As I stood by the ocean, enveloped in the vastness of God's creation, I found solace in prayer and reflection.

The waves crashing against the shore echoed the magnitude of God's power and sovereignty, instilling in me a renewed sense of awe and reverence. In that moment of communion with the divine, I felt a profound sense of peace and reassurance, knowing that God's love transcended all earthly trials and tribulations. Later, during a church service at Victory Praise Centre, I received a prophetic word affirming God's calling on my life. The pastor's wife singled me out, speaking words of encouragement and affirmation that resonated deeply within my spirit. Her message served as a confirmation of God's faithfulness and provision, reaffirming my commitment to His divine purpose.

Navigating Distractions

Despite the accolades and spiritual experiences, I faced moments of doubt and distraction as I grappled with the pressures of ministry and public speaking. A particularly challenging sermon left me questioning my abilities and effectiveness as a speaker, prompting feelings of inadequacy and self-doubt. However, a surprising gesture of gratitude from a member of the congregation served as a reminder of God's ability to work through imperfect vessels, restoring my faith and confidence in His plan. Through the highs and lows of my journey in Northern Ireland, I learned valuable lessons about faith, resilience, and the transformative power of God's love.

Each encounter, whether with journalists, disruptive students, or divine billboards, served to deepen my understanding of God's sovereignty and His unwavering presence in my life. As I continued to navigate the challenges and opportunities before me, I remained steadfast in my commitment to fulfilling God's calling and sharing His love with others.

CHAPTER 10

Return to Zimbabwe

"It always seems impossible until it's done."
-Nelson Mandela

Returning to Zimbabwe after a year in Northern Ireland was a bittersweet experience. Leaving behind the comforts of my newfound family was difficult, but my work there had been accomplished, marking the end of a significant chapter in my life. As I bid farewell to my loved ones, tears streamed down my cheeks, a testament to the deep connections forged during my time abroad.

Stepping off the plane in Harare, I felt a mix of excitement and apprehension about returning to familiar surroundings. Meeting with the National Director of SU upon my arrival brought a sense of reassurance, knowing that my journey in Zimbabwe would continue with purpose. Upon my arrival at Harare International Airport, I was warmly welcomed by Simba Takawira from Scripture Union, signaling the start of a new phase of my ministry journey. From there, I was taken to the Scripture Union headquarters where I had the privilege of meeting Paul Revel, a mentor whose influence would profoundly impact my Christian faith.

Paul and his wife Ellen opened their home to me, providing a nurturing environment where I continued to grow spiritually. Their exemplary lives of devotion to Christ served as a constant source of inspiration and challenge for me to deepen my walk with God.

Paul Revel, in addition to his pastoral responsibilities at the Covenanters in Mabelreign, also served as the Administrator of Scripture Union Northern Region. Under his guidance, I found myself drawn into a deeper understanding of Scripture and a renewed commitment to living out my faith in practical ways. His emphasis on the importance of reading the Bible and being a bold witness for Christ left a lasting impression on me, shaping the trajectory of my ministry journey.

FROM STRUGGLE TO STRENGTH: THE JOURNEY OF A REVEREND

Another significant figure I encountered upon my return was Mkoma Tim Tavaziva, the Director of Scripture Union Northern Region. Initially, I perceived him as stern and difficult, but as I got to know him better, I discovered his true character – a man grounded in Scripture, humble, and compassionate. Mkoma Tim's willingness to sit on the floor during a visit to my humble dwelling in Budiriro spoke volumes about his servant-hearted nature. His prayers and words of encouragement instilled in me a sense of hope and resilience, reminding me of God's faithfulness even in adversity.

Arriving in Budiriro, my family welcomed me home with open arms, but the reality of readjusting to life in Zimbabwe soon set in. Sleeping on a sofa on my first night back was a stark contrast to the comfort I had grown accustomed to, signaling the beginning of a new chapter filled with cultural adjustments and challenges.

Engaging with the church community in Budiriro, I soon realized that this was where I was meant to be. Drawing from my ministerial experience, I took on the role of Youth Pastor, leading both the church's youth and the wider community through a ministry called Youth Life Agenda. This interdenominational youth group provided a platform for young people to address the challenges they faced in a supportive and participatory environment.

CHAPTER 11

Meeting my wife

"When love is the way, we will let justice roll down like a mighty stream and righteousness like an ever-flowing brook." -Bell Hooks

Among the many lives touched by our ministry was a young lady named Winterpet, whose dedication and commitment left a lasting impression. Our shared passion for the ministry eventually blossomed into a deeper connection, and on December 5, 1998, we embarked on a new journey together, united in love and faith.

As I settled back into life in Zimbabwe and began my full-time role with Scripture Union, I carried with me the lessons learned and the friendships forged during my time abroad. Each encounter, whether with mentors like Paul Revel and Mkoma Tim or with colleagues and friends, served to deepen my understanding of God's calling on my life and reaffirmed my commitment to serving Him wholeheartedly. The journey ahead was uncertain, but with faith as my compass and the support of a strong Christian community, I embraced the challenges and opportunities that lay ahead, trusting in God's provision and guidance every step of the way.

As my journey continued, I found myself expanding my horizons in both my personal and professional life. Marrying Winterpet was just the beginning of a new chapter filled with blessings and opportunities. Together, we embarked on a journey of faith and growth, supporting each other through life's challenges and celebrations.

In my career with Scripture Union, I found fulfillment in serving the community and spreading the message of Christ's love. Working as a field officer in High Glen, I collaborated with a dedicated team of S.U advisors to organize impactful events and rallies that brought together young people from diverse backgrounds. One memorable event was a gospel rally at Domboshawa Mountain, where over a thousand youth gathered to worship and hear the word of God.

These experiences were a testament to the transformative power of faith and community. Under the guidance of Mr. Kudakwashe Gwemende, my supervisor at S.U Northern Region, I continued to grow professionally and spiritually. Mr. Gwemende's integrity and support bolstered my confidence and commitment to my work. His mentorship paved the way for significant achievements, including organizing stakeholder meetings and receiving a scholarship to pursue further studies in theology.

Driven by a desire for knowledge and personal development, I seized the opportunity to pursue higher education. With the support of Dr. Phineas Dube, the National Director of Scripture Union, I embarked on a journey to obtain a degree in Theology from Zimbabwe Open University. This academic pursuit broadened my understanding of scripture and equipped me with valuable insights to serve God's purpose more effectively.

In addition to my theological studies, I pursued a Master's degree in Business Leadership and Management from the National University of Science and Technology (NUST). This multidisciplinary approach to education empowered me to integrate faith and leadership principles into my professional endeavors, fostering a holistic approach to ministry and community development. Amidst my academic pursuits, Winterpet and I welcomed two children into our family: Righteous Inzwirashe and Kaylie Makatendeishe. Their presence brought immeasurable joy and deepened our sense of gratitude for God's blessings. Together, we strive to instill values of faith, integrity, and service in our children, nurturing them to become compassionate and purpose-driven individuals. As I reflect on my journey, I am reminded of the transformative power of faith and the importance of steadfast perseverance in the face of adversity. From humble beginnings in rural Zimbabwe to academic and professional achievements beyond my wildest dreams, I am humbled by God's faithfulness and grace.

This book serves as a testament to God's redemptive love and His ability to transform lives. I hope that through sharing my story, others may find inspiration and encouragement to trust in God's plan for their lives, knowing that with faith, all things are possible.

CHAPTER 12

The Art of Worship and Fasting

Missions exist because worship doesn't- John Piper

In the quest for spiritual fulfillment, my journey has been intertwined with the disciplines of worship and fasting, forming the bedrock of my spiritual growth. From my early days in Shamva, where I grappled with the dichotomy between my newfound faith and the heinous activities around me, to the present, these disciplines have remained integral to my walk with God.

Prayer and worship serve as conduits for communication with the divine. As Jesus taught His disciples, prayer is not merely a ritual but a means of establishing a connection with God. Through prayer, I have delved deeper into my relationship with the divine, seeking His guidance and wisdom in times of joy and sorrow alike. Fasting, on the other hand, is a discipline that transcends the physical realm, allowing for a separation of self from the distractions of the world. By abstaining from food and worldly pleasures, one can silence the voice of the flesh and attune oneself to the voice of God. Fasting has become a cornerstone of my spiritual journey, a practice I adhere to on a regular basis to draw closer to the divine.

Worship, intertwined with prayer and fasting, is an essential aspect of my spiritual life. Through worship, I glorify God for His goodness and magnify His presence in my life. Whether through music or silent reverence, worship allows me to express my gratitude and adoration for the divine. It is in moments of worship that I find solace and peace, as I bask in the presence of the Almighty.

Yet, worship is not confined to the sanctuary; it permeates every aspect of my existence. From the strumming of a guitar to the joyous dance of celebration, worship is a continuous expression of my faith and devotion. It is through worship that I testify to God's faithfulness and proclaim His glory to the world. In the realm of worship and fasting, I have found solace, strength, and spiritual sustenance. These disciplines have shaped my journey of faith, guiding me through the trials and triumphs of life. As I continue to walk this path, I am reminded of the words of the Psalmist: "Taste and see that the Lord is good; blessed is the one who takes refuge in him." (Psalm 34:8).

CONCLUSION

As we reach the conclusion of this book, I am filled with a profound sense of gratitude and awe at the journey we have undertaken together. From the humble beginnings in rural Zimbabwe to the triumphs and challenges faced along the way, "Mission Impossible: Reconstructing" has been a testament to the resilience of the human spirit and the transformative power of faith. Throughout the pages of this book, we have encountered numerous lessons and reflections that have shaped our understanding of life, faith, and the human experience. From the importance of perseverance and determination in the face of adversity to the profound impact of love, community, and faith, each chapter has offered valuable insights into the complexities of the human journey. One of the most profound lessons we have learned is the importance of embracing our struggles and allowing them to shape us into stronger, more resilient individuals. In every challenge we face, there is an opportunity for growth and transformation, if only we have the courage to persevere. We have also been reminded of the incredible power of faith to sustain us through the darkest of times and to guide us towards a brighter future.

No matter how daunting the obstacles may seem, we can take comfort in the knowledge that we are never alone, for God is always by our side, offering strength, comfort, and guidance. But perhaps the most important lesson of all is the importance of love—love for ourselves, love for one another, and love for God. It is love that sustains us in our darkest hours, that binds us together as a community, and that ultimately gives meaning and purpose to our lives. As we close this chapter of our lives and prepare to embark on the next, let us carry forward these lessons and reflections with us. Let us continue to walk in faith, to embrace our struggles with courage and determination, and to live each day with love and gratitude in our hearts. Thank you for being a part of this incredible journey. May God bless you abundantly, now and always.

Don't miss out!

Visit the website below and you can sign up to receive emails whenever Rev Maxwell Ngove publishes a new book. There's no charge and no obligation.

https://books2read.com/r/B-A-YVLPB-EBASD

About the Author

Maxwell Ngove, a revered figure in Zimbabwe holds the esteemed title of Reverend, a testament to his unwavering commitment to his faith, Ordained with reverence, Maxwell's life is a testament to his dedication to serving others, primarily through his profound involvement with Scripture Union, where he discovered his calling in ministering to the youth. As a devoted family man, Maxwell is blessed with two children, a son and a daughter, and shares a joyous union with his wife, Winterpet Ngove, in Mutare Zimbabwe. With wealth of leadership experience and a fervent passion for philanthropy, Maxwell excels in personnel management, strategic planning, and team development. He tenures as a Provincial Coordinator for Scripture Union Zimbabwe exemplifies his adaptness in overseeing programs., spearheading fundraising initiatives, and naturing staff development. Maxwell's comitment to education is palpable in his academic accolades, boasting a Bachelor of Arts degree in Theology and a Master's degree in Leadership and

Management. Presently Maxwell is deeply engaged in the education of young minds, particulalry in matters of spirituality and the teachings of God. Through his tireless work and steadfast pursuit of knowledge, Maxwell continues to inspire others to harness their potential to make a meaningful contributions to the world, "From Struggle to Strength" encapsulates Maxwell's transformative journey-a journey of faith, resilience, and unwavering dedication to serving others.

www.ingramcontent.com/pod-product-compliance
Lightning Source LLC
Chambersburg PA
CBHW072209090426
42740CB00012B/2458
* 9 7 8 0 7 9 6 1 5 4 4 6 0 *